Shut Up & Colour This Shit 2: INSULTS

A Swear Word Adult Colouring Book

Georgina Townsend

Shut Up & Colour This Shit 2: INSULTS A Swear Word Adult Colouring Book
Edited by Georgina Townsend

Published by Ravensforge Books

ISBN: 978-1-912325-07-8

THIS IS A TEST PAGE, PLEASE FEEL FREE TO TRY OUT YOUR MATERIALS

THIS IS A TEST PAGE, PLEASE FEEL FREE TO TRY OUT YOUR MATERIALS

Boob Banger

EXPURR-IMENTAL PUSSY

FUCK THIS NOISE

CRAB-TICKLER

SHEEP-SHAGGER

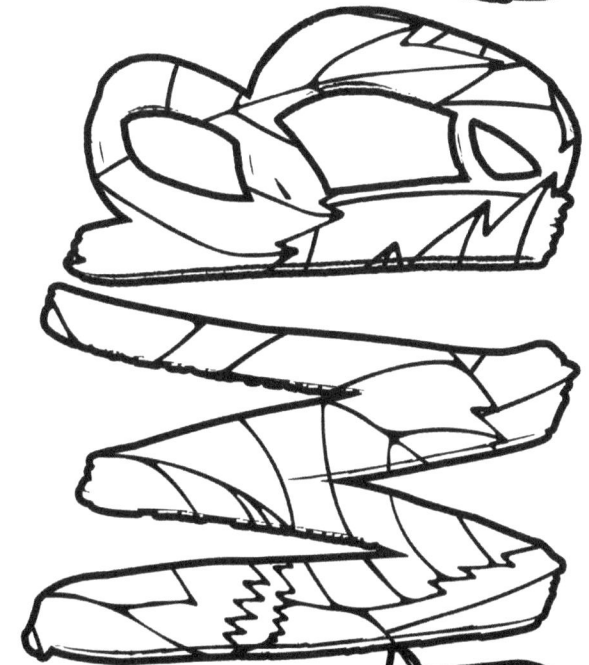

Arse Gravy

YER...

BERK

BUBLE...

DINGBAT

Flange Flicker

Turd Farmer

DONUT PUNCHER

Dolphin Vagina

piefucker

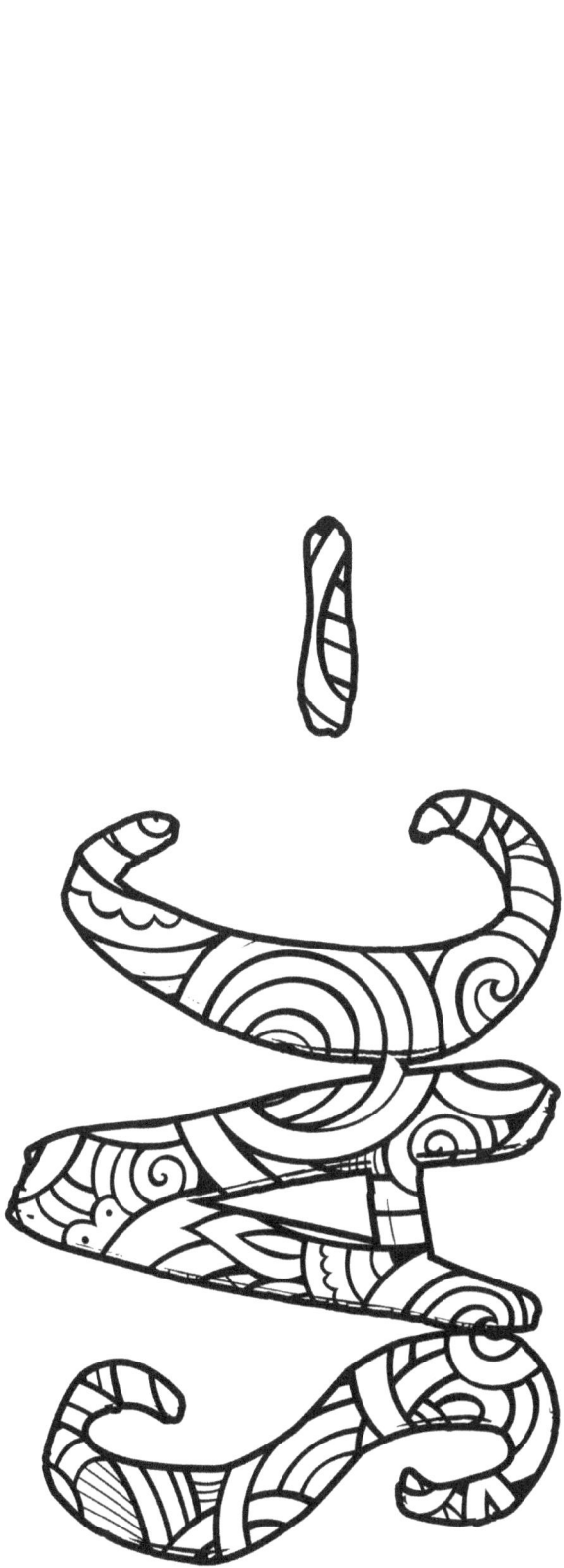

BELLEND

FLAP-
ITCH

I CANNOT CANNOT CAN'T

RIMJOB

MUTHACLUCKER

COCK
JOCKEY

MUTHACLUCKER

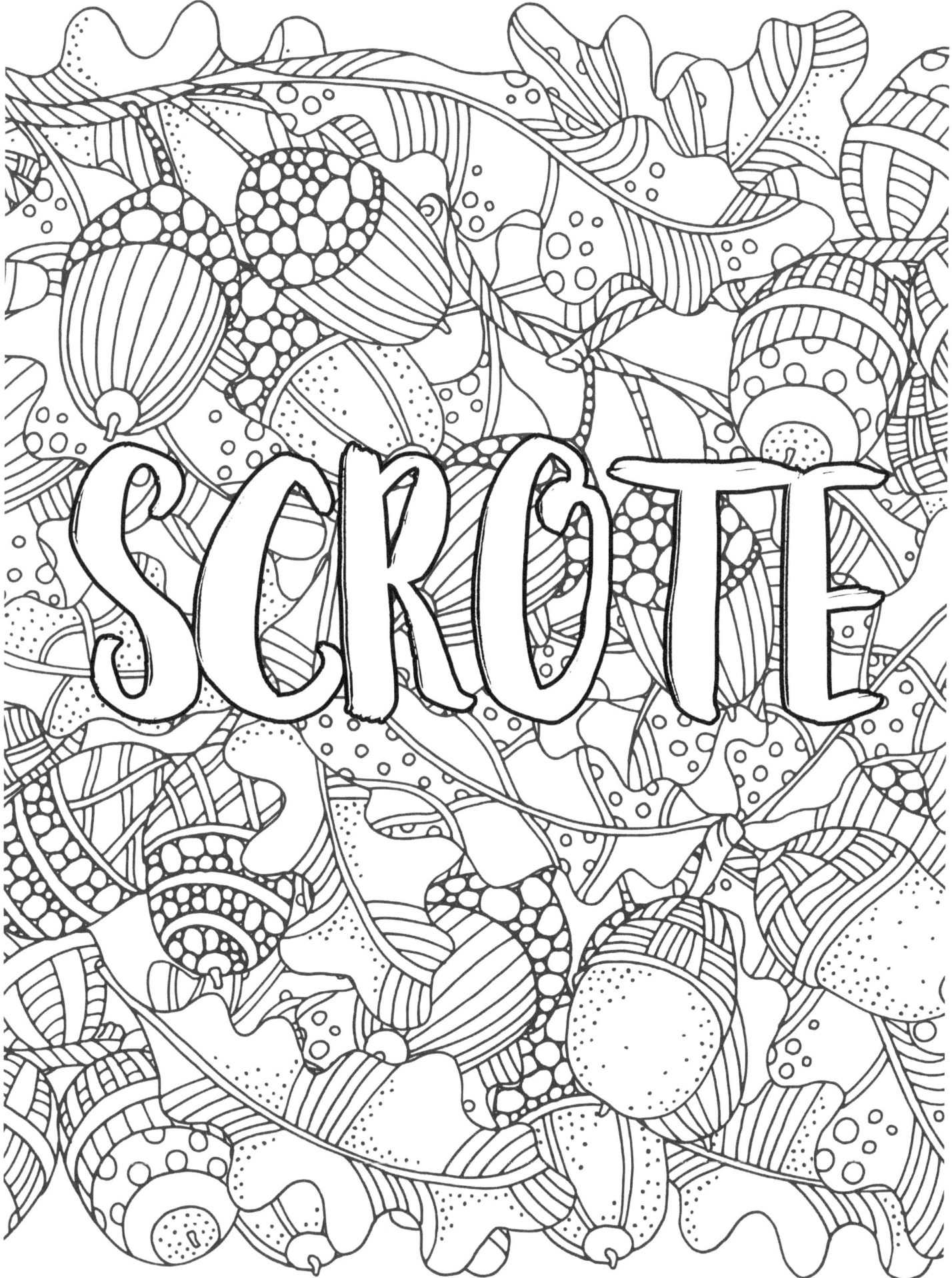

SCROTE

PUKE
MONGER

SPUNK-STRUMMER

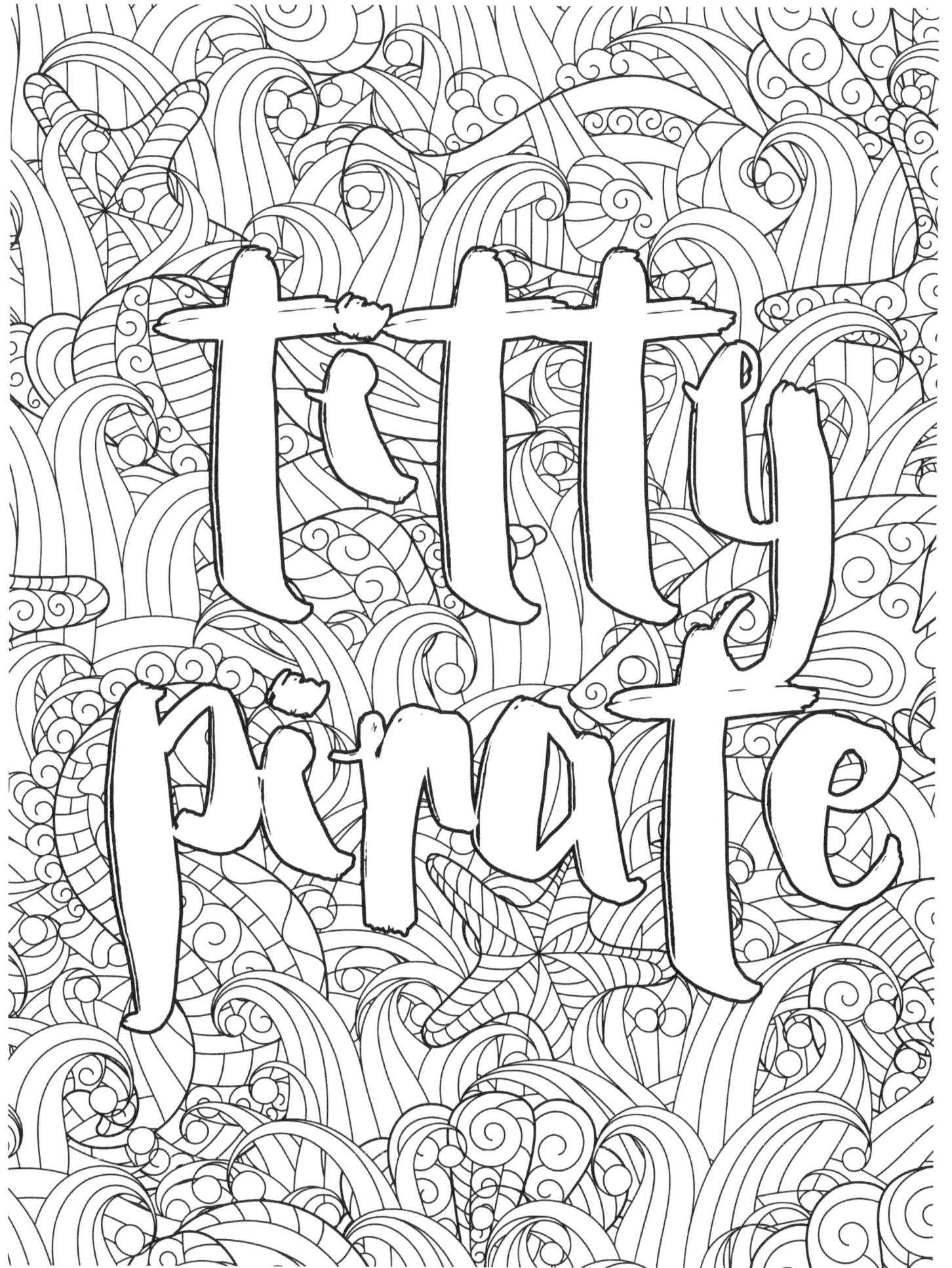

titty pirate

Thanks for colouring! If you would like to discover more adult colouring books in our range, you can find us on Amazon or at ravensforgebooks.com

Other titles from Ravensforge Books include:

Shut Up & Colour This Shit: A Swear Word Adult Colouring Book
Edited by Georgina Townsend

*

Shut Up & Colour This Shit: A Swear Word Adult Colouring Book
LEFT-HANDED edition
Edited by Georgina Townsend

*

Shut Up & Colour This Shit: A TRAVEL-SIZE Swear Word Adult Colouring
Edited by Georgina Townsend

*

Shut Up & Colour This Shit 2: Insults - A Swear Word Adult Colouring Book
LEFT-HANDED Edition
Edited by Georgina Townsend

*

Shut Up & Colour This Shit 2: Insults - A TRAVEL-SIZE Swear Word
Adult Colouring Book
Edited by Georgina Townsend

*

Ocean Dreams: A Nautical-Themed Adult Colouring Book
Edited by Georgina Townsend

*

Dinosaur Days: A Prehistoric-Themed Adult Colouring Book
Edited by Georgina Townsend

*

Ancient Worlds: A Historic-Themed Adult Colouring Book
Edited by Georgina Townsend

*

Country Calm: A Countryside-Themed Adult Colouring Book
Edited by Georgina Townsend

*

Fantasy Magic: A Fantasy-Themed Adult Colouring Book
Edited by Georgina Townsend

*

Cat Capers: A Kitty-Themed Adult Colouring Book
Edited by Georgina Townsend

www.ingramcontent.com/pod-product-compliance
Lightning Source LLC
Chambersburg PA
CBHW081241020426

42331CB00013B/3251